ESL
CONTENT-BASED LANGUAGE
Games, Puzzles, and Inventive Exercises

by Imogene Forte
and Mary Ann Pangle

Incentive Publications, Inc.
Nashville, Tennessee

Illustrated by Marta Drayton
Cover by Marta Drayton
Edited by Jean K. Signor

ISBN 978-0-86530-487-1

3   4   5   6   7   8   9   10   11   10   09   08

PRINTED IN THE UNITED STATES OF AMERICA
www.incentivepublications.com

Table of Contents

HOW TO USE THIS BOOK

Learning is the focal point of the activities included in <u>ESL Content-Based Language Games, Puzzles, and Inventive Exercises</u>, and the content-based nature of the exercises ensures that students are learning more than English. This book will be a valuable tool for all teachers who work with students learning English as a second language (ESL); the books in this series will be helpful for or with students needing additional reinforcement with acquisition of basic language skills.

Each activity is content-based to develop language concepts and strategies connected to a specific subject. Additionally, the exercises in this book offer opportunities for learning, practicing, and mastery of a variety of essential language-based skills. Each exercise includes a list of materials, preparation directions, and player directions. Many exercises have accompanying reproducible activity sheets for immediate classroom skill and/or concept reinforcement. A skills checklist with correlations to exercises designed to reinforce the skill, a suggested bibliography for additional references, and an answer key are also provided. These tools are designed to help teachers plan their lessons and track the achievement of their students. Each lesson is designed for use by ESL students at widely varying age and grade levels.

Students need to use learned material, and practice plays an essential role in the mastery and retention of any skill or concept. In addition to individual worksheets, many exercises provide activities that promote cooperative learning and peer tutoring. Cooperative learning activities are essential in an ESL classroom as they enable students to work collaboratively to verbalize, refine, and process newly-acquired knowledge and skills. The themes of high interest on which these activities are based will further encourage student interaction and communication.

This book was written with an eye on the Cognitive Academic Language Learning Approach (CALLA). Accordingly, the exercises encourage the four major conditions of this teaching method: first, to foster a learning environment of high expectations; secondly, to create opportunities to integrate language development with content-based instruction; thirdly, to provide support for teachers in the classroom; and finally, to demonstrate assessment options that empower teachers to plan effective lessons for their students.

The games, puzzles, and exercises within <u>ESL Content-Based Language Games, Puzzles, and Inventive Exercises</u> will help teachers make the most effective use of their time in helping their ESL students to learn essential content-based skills, improve their use of the English language, and acquire problem-solving skills and concepts important to student success.

Essential Language Skills Checklist
and
Correlations to Activity Titles

ESL Content-Based Language Games, Puzzles, and Inventive Exercises

Skills Exercises

Time on the Line

Purpose:
    Math - telling time
    Language - vocabulary, speaking, decision making

Materials:
    Math cube for a marker
    Copy of the game board

Number of Players:
    Two

Preparation Directions:
1. Review telling time with the students.
2. Give a copy of the game board to the players.
3. Write the numbers 1 and 2 with a black marker on the sides of a math cube.

Player Directions:
1. The first player throws the math cube and moves the correct number of spaces.
2. The player must say the correct time that is written on the clock in the space.
3. If the player says the incorrect time, he or she must go back one space.
4. The game continues until one player reaches "FINISH" and wins the game.

Bonus Activity:

Provide drawing paper and crayons and ask students to draw a clock face marked to show the time they get up, the time school begins, the time they eat lunch, and the time they go to bed. Exhibit the completed drawings on a bulletin board.

Time on the Line Game Board

*ESL Content-Based Language
Games, Puzzles, and Inventive Exercises*

Pizza Problems

Purpose:
    Math - addition, subtraction, multiplication, and division; number practice
    Language - writing, decision-making, discussion

Materials:
    Copies of game boards
    Scissors
    Pencils
    Clock

Number of Players:
    Two

Preparation Directions:

1. Distribute copies of the game boards.

2. Ask each player to cut the addition and subtraction pizza into four pieces.

3. Ask each player to cut the multiplication and division pizza into four pieces.

4. Provide pencils.

5. Place a clock in an easily accessible spot.

Player Directions:

1. Each player takes one piece of the addition and subtraction pizza and places it face down.

2. The players look at the clock and write the time on the back of the piece of pizza.

3. At a given signal, the players turn the piece of pizza over and write the answers to the problems.

4. The game continues until all of the answers on the four addition and subtraction pizza pieces have been completed.

5. The player who finishes in the least amount of time and has the correct answers wins the game.

6. The multiplication and division pizza worksheets may be used to play the game again.

7. A class discussion related to different kinds of pizzas, their cost, nutritional value, and a graph showing student favorites will provide helpful health and nutritional information in a timely manner.

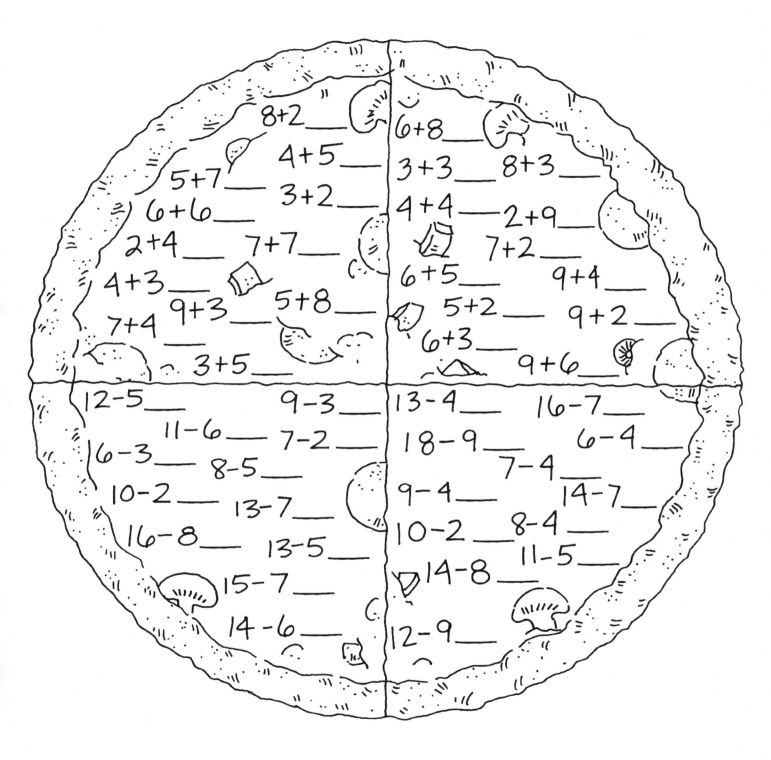

8+2 ___
4+5 ___
5+7 ___
3+2 ___
6+6 ___
2+4 ___   7+7 ___
4+3 ___
7+4   9+3 ___   5+8 ___
3+5 ___

6+8 ___
3+3 ___   8+3 ___
4+4 ___   2+9 ___
7+2 ___
6+5 ___   9+4 ___
5+2 ___   9+2 ___
6+3 ___
9+6 ___

12-5 ___   9-3 ___
11-6 ___   7-2 ___
6-3 ___   8-5 ___
10-2 ___   13-7 ___
16-8 ___   13-5 ___
15-7 ___
14-6 ___

13-4 ___   16-7 ___
18-9 ___   6-4 ___
7-4 ___
9-4 ___   14-7 ___
10-2 ___   8-4 ___
14-8 ___   11-5 ___
12-9 ___

13

4 × 8 ____

5 × 5 ____   2 × 9 ____

6 × 3 ____   3 × 9 ____

3 × 4 ____

9 × 6 ____

7 × 4 ____   6 × 5 ____

7 × 8 ____   4 × 4 ____

3 × 3 ____

3 × 7 ____

9 × 9 ____   6 × 4 ____

4 × 9 ____   6 × 8 ____

2 × 6 ____

3 × 10 ____   5 × 7 ____

8 × 3 ____   8 × 5 ____

9 × 7 ____

4 × 2 ____

81 ÷ 9 ____   24 ÷ 6 ____

27 ÷ 3 ____   18 ÷ 6 ____

9 ÷ 3 ____   8 ÷ 2 ____

42 ÷ 6 ____   56 ÷ 8 ____

6 ÷ 2 ____   21 ÷ 3 ____

45 ÷ 9 ____

64 ÷ 8 ____

36 ÷ 9 ____   15 ÷ 3 ____

16 ÷ 2 ____   27 ÷ 9 ____

36 ÷ 6 ____   28 ÷ 4 ____

30 ÷ 6 ____

14 ÷ 2 ____   35 ÷ 5 ____

63 ÷ 9 ____

12 ÷ 4 ____

16 ÷ 4 ____

Orange Orchard

Purpose:

Math - counting, rank order

Language - reading and following directions, descriptive words

Materials:

Copy of Maze

Follow-up activity

Pencils

Crayons

Number of Players:

One or the entire class

Preparation Directions:

1. Distribute copies of the maze and a copy of the follow-up activity sheet.

2. Provide pencils and crayons

Player Directions:

1. The player or players follow the directions on the maze.

2. After completing the maze, the player or players follow the directions on the follow-up activity.

Bonus Activity:

Provide an orange for each member of the class. Ask students to place the orange in front of them and look at it closely, turn it over and over in their hands, feel it, smell it, and of course eat it. During this exercise, ask them to name words that describe the orange. As the words are named, write them on a chart or chalkboard. When the list is completed, read the entire list and ask students to rank order the six words that best describe the orange.

Orange Orchard

Count the oranges as you follow the maze.

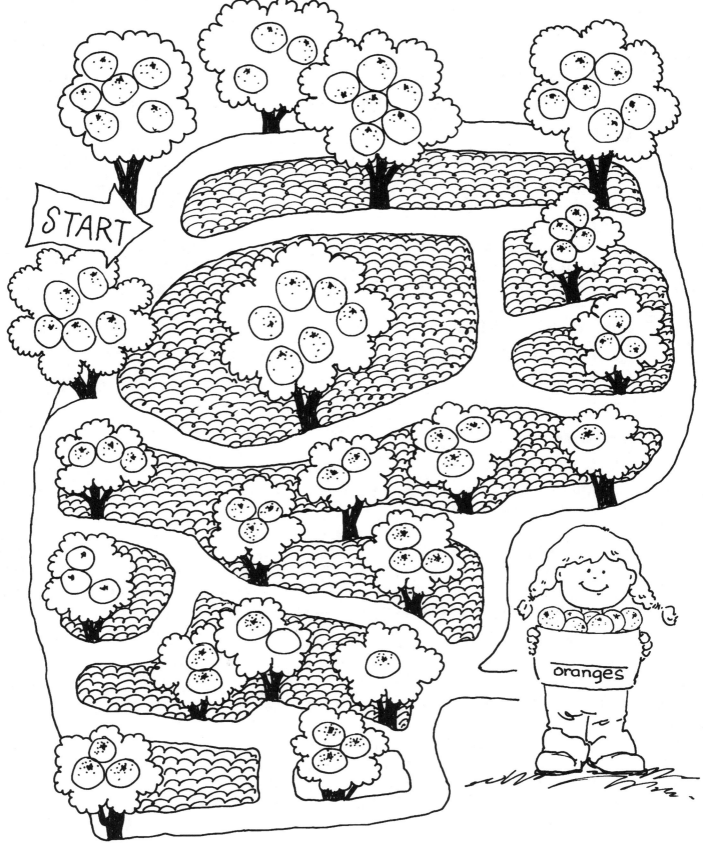

Orange Orchard Follow-up Activity

Count the oranges in the baskets.

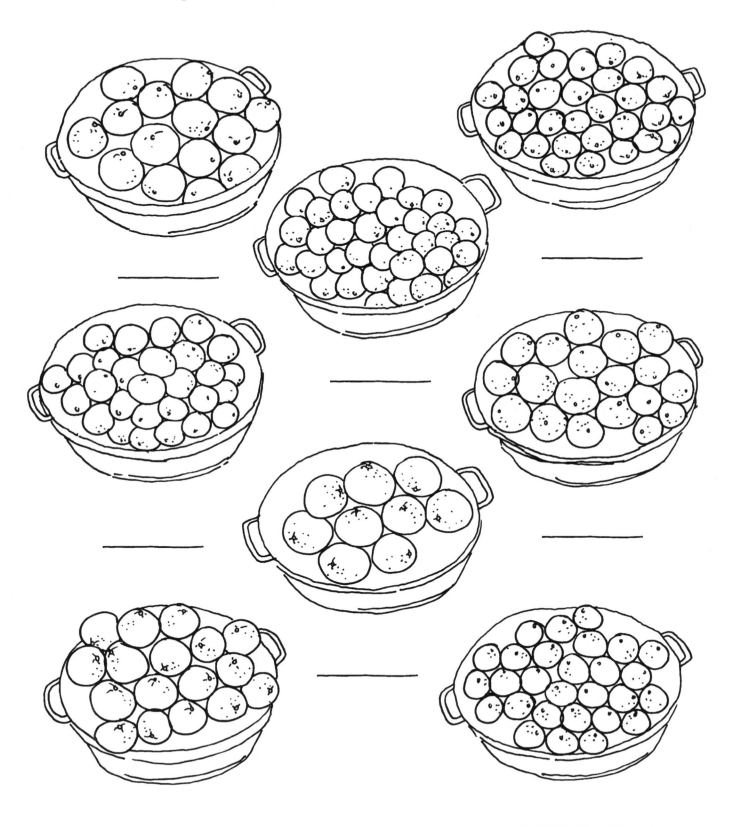

ESL Content-Based Language
Games, Puzzles, and Inventive Exercises

Odd and Even Jelly Beans

Purpose:

    Math - odd and even number practice

    Language - following directions, listening, rhyming words

Materials:

    Jelly Bean Activity Sheet

    Crayons

Number of Players:

    Whole class or small groups

Preparation Directions:

    1. Give each player a Jelly Bean Activity Sheet.

    2. Provide crayons for each player.

Player Directions:

    1. The players color the even-numbered jelly beans yellow.

    2. Then the players color the odd-numbered jelly beans green.

Bonus Activity:

Play a jelly bean rhyme game. Have students sit in a circle. Pass out different colored jelly beans, one to each student.

The first player begins the game by turning to the person on his or her right, naming the color of his or her jelly bean and supplying an additional sentence ending with a word that rhymes with the color word. Example: "My jelly bean is red. It is time for bed." If the rhyming word sentence is correctly supplied, the player receives an additional jelly bean.

The next player takes a turn and so on around the circle. When a sentence ending with the rhyming word cannot be supplied, that player drops out of the game. The game continues with each player left in the game taking a new term and using the color of the last jelly bean supplied. The last player left in the game is declared the winner of the game.

Odd and Even Jelly Beans Activity Sheet

Color the even-numbered jelly beans yellow.
Color the odd-numbered jelly beans green.

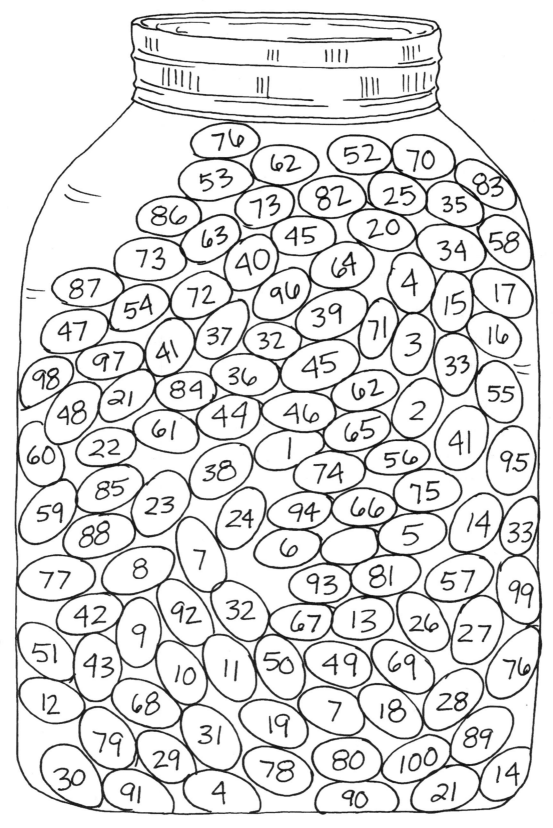

*ESL Content-Based Language
Games, Puzzles, and Inventive Exercises*

Space Craft

Purpose:
>   **Math** - counting
>   **Language** - reading and following directions

Materials:
>   Copy of Maze
>   Follow-up activity
>   Pencils
>   Crayons

Number of Players:
>   One or the entire class

Preparation Directions:

1. Provide copies of the maze and the follow-up activity sheet.

2. Provide pencils and crayons

Player Directions:

1. The player or players follow the directions on the maze.

2. After completing the maze, the player or players follow the directions to complete the follow-up activity.

Space Craft

Follow the maze to reach the moon.

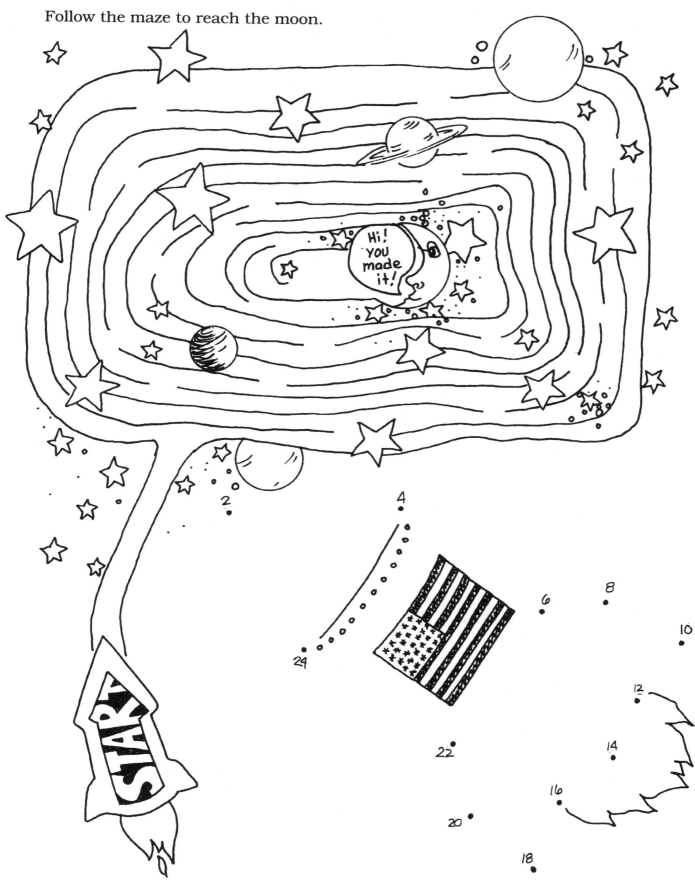

ESL Content-Based Language
Games, Puzzles, and Inventive Exercises

Follow the Numbers

Purpose:

    Math Skills - counting by fives

    Language - following directions, titles, story writing, oral reading

Materials:

    Copy of game board

    Crayons

    Pencils

Number of Players:

    A whole class, one, or two Players

Preparation Directions:

1. Distribute copies of the game board worksheet.
2. Provide a pencil and crayons for each player.

Player Directions:

1. The players visit the zoo by completing the maze activity.
2. The players enter the zoo and begin at 0.
3. Then the players use a pencil to travel through the maze counting by 5's to 100 in order.
4. After completing the maze, the players may color the zoo animals.

Bonus Activity:

Ask students to write an original story by using one of the following titles:

… The Day the Tiger Escaped from his Pen

… The Most Interesting Animal in the Zoo

… My Adventure at the Zoo

… The Zoo's Newest Resident, a New Elephant

Discuss nouns and ask the students to underline all the nouns in their stories.

Provide time for each student to read his or her story aloud to the class.

Follow the Numbers

Follow the numbers to trace the path you took to see the animals.

TIGERS

25

ELEPHANT

30

20

15

35

ZOO

10

80

75

ENTRANCE   5   40

MONKEY

ZEBRAS

45

70

50

65

60

95

85

90

55

100

EXIT

ESL Content-Based Language
Games, Puzzles, and Inventive Exercises

Calendar Clues

Purpose:
Math - calendar counting
Language - locating information, vocabulary

Materials:
Copy of the calendar
Copy of the game cards
Copy of the activity sheet
Scissors
Pencils

Number of Players:
Two

Preparation Directions:
1. Distribute copies of the calendar and the accompanying worksheet.
2. Provide pencils.
3. Ask students to cut out the game cards.

Player Directions:
1. The month in which the game is being played is used to complete the calendar.
2. The cards are shuffled and placed face down.
3. The first player draws a card, reads, and answers the question orally.
4. Then both of the players write the answer to the question beside the correct number on the activity sheet.
5. The game continues until all of the questions have been answered.

Calendar Clues Monthly Calendar

SATURDAY					
FRIDAY					
THURSDAY					
WEDNESDAY					
TUESDAY					
MONDAY					
SUNDAY					

ESL Content-Based Language
Games, Puzzles, and Inventive Exercises

Calendar Clues Game Cards

1.

What will be the date a week from the 3rd?

2.

List the dates of all the Tuesdays.

3.

How many days are there between the 10th and the 24th? How many weeks?

4.

On the 29th, what was the date two weeks ago?

5.

How many school days are in the month?

6.

If today is the 7th, what is the date for the day before yesterday? What is the day of the week?

7.

What day of the week will the first day of the next month be?

8.

If today is the 17th, what will be the day after tomorrow? What is the day of the week?

9.

How many days are there from the 2nd to the 23rd? How many weeks?

10.

How many Saturdays are there in the month? List the dates for the Saturdays.

11.

Find out how many students in your class have a birthday in this month. List the dates of the birthdays.

12.

Count backwards from the 25th to the 4th. How many days will this be? How many weeks?

Calendar Clues Activity Sheet

How many days are in a week? _____

How many months are in a year? _____

Use the cards to answer the questions.

1. _____

2. _____

3. _____   _____

4. _____

5. _____

6. _____   _____

7. _____

8. _____   _____

9. _____   _____

10. _____   _____

11. _____   _____

12. _____   _____

*ESL Content-Based Language
Games, Puzzles, and Inventive Exercises*

Number Land

Purpose:
  Math skills and number practice

Materials:
  Copy of game board
  Scissors
  Copy of game cards
  Game markers

Number of Players:
  Two or Four

Preparation Directions:

1. Distribute copies of the game board and game cards.

2. Distribute a game marker to each player.

3. Direct groups to cut out the game cards.

Player Directions:

1. The game cards are shuffled and placed face down.

2. The first player draws a card and reads it.

3. If the player gets the correct answer to the math problem on the card, he or she moves one space.

4. Then the other players take turns drawing cards and solving their own math problems.

5. The game continues until one player reaches "Finish" and wins the game.

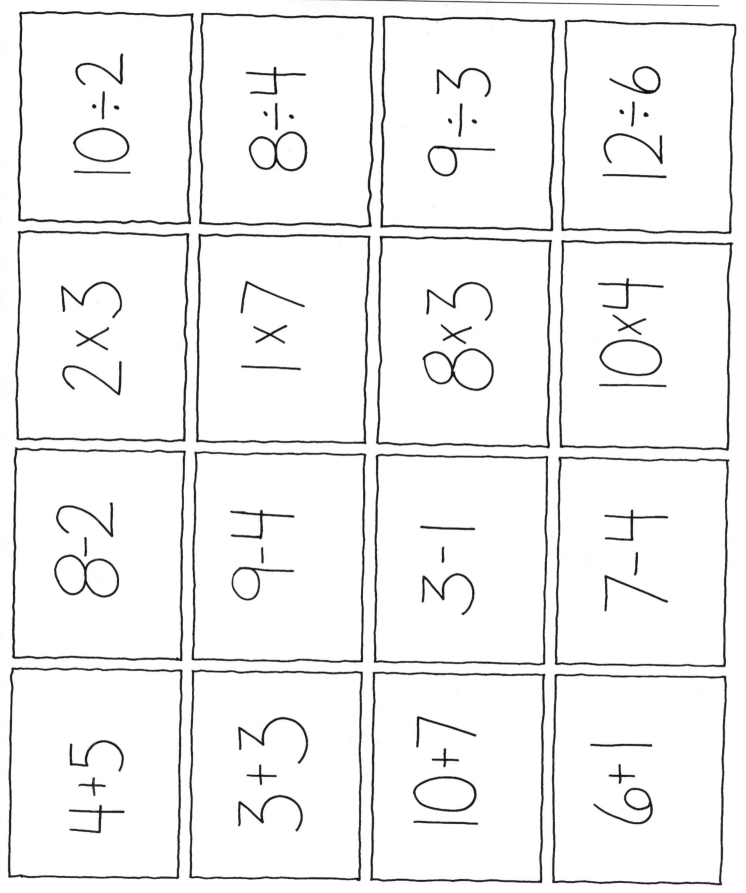

*ESL Content-Based Language
Games, Puzzles, and Inventive Exercises*

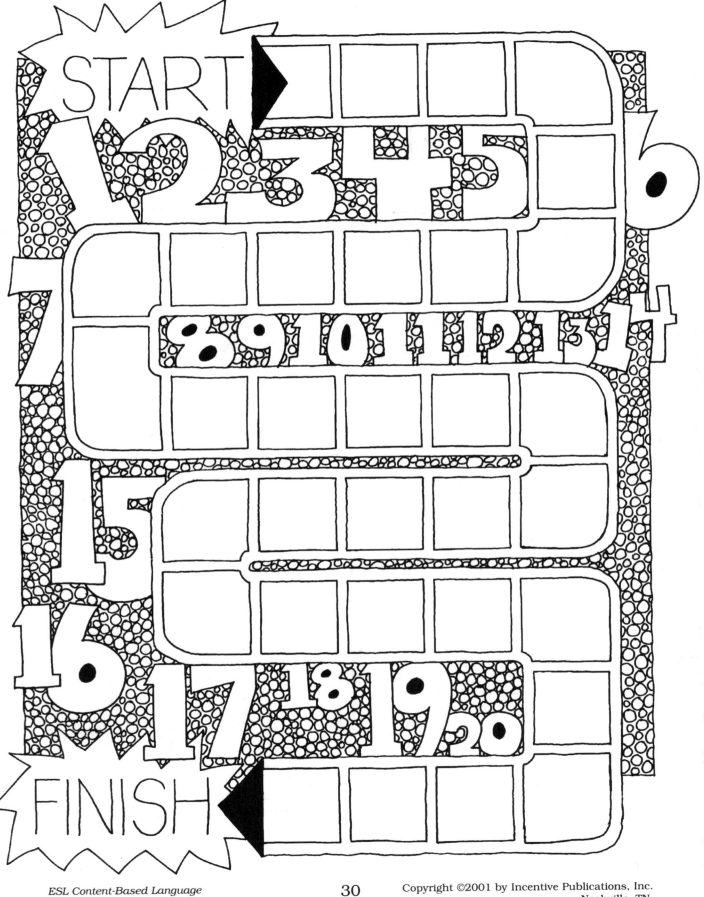

START
1 2 3 4 5 6
7
8 9 10 11 12 13 14
15
16 17 18 19 20
FINISH

Hamburger House

Purpose:

    Math - money

    Language - reading and following directions, vocabulary

Materials:

    Copy of Maze

    Copy of Follow-up activity

    Pencils

    Crayons

Number of Players:

    One or the entire class

Preparation Directions:

1. Distribute copies of the maze and the follow-up activity sheet.

2. Provide pencils and crayons

Player Directions:

1. The player or players follow the directions on the maze.

2. After completing the maze, the player or players follow the directions to complete the follow-up activity.

Hamburger House

Follow the maze
to the Hamburger House.

Order a meal at the Hamburger House.

Add up the prices to find out how much your entire meal will cost.

Write the name of each food and how much it will cost.

Draw a picture of each food.

HAMBURGER HOUSE

DATE: _____ SERVER: _____

NAME OF FOOD	PRICE
Hamburger	75¢
Milk	35¢
Chips	35¢
Cookie	25¢
TOTAL:	

Thanks!

Sign Savvy

Purpose:

Social Studies - recognizing signs

Language: word recognition, vocabulary enrichment, recalling previously learned information

Materials:

Copy of game board

Markers

Game cards

Scissors

Number of Players:

Two

Preparation Directions:

1. Distribute copies of the game board and game cards.

2. Instruct the groups to cut out the game cards and markers.

Player Directions:

1. The game cards are shuffled and placed face down.

2. The players place the markers on "Start."

3. The first player draws a card and follows the directions that are written on it.

4. The player must say the name of the sign that is written on the space.

5. If the player cannot identify the sign, he or she must move back one space.

6. Taking turns, the game continues until one player reaches "Finish" and wins the game.

STOP STOP

MOVE ONE SPACE

MOVE TWO SPACES

LOSE ONE TURN

GO BACK ONE SPACE

MOVE ONE SPACE AND TAKE ANOTHER TURN

MOVE ONE SPACE

Is this sign used in your native country?

MOVE ONE SPACE

What color is this sign?

MOVE ONE SPACE

Where have you seen this sign?

*ESL Content-Based Language
Games, Puzzles, and Inventive Exercises*

ESL Content-Based Language Games, Puzzles, and Inventive Exercises

Monthly Madness

Purpose:

Social Studies - numbers, calendar

Language Arts - words in context, sight words, paragraph writing, abbreviations

Materials:

Copy of game activities

Pencils

Scissors

Paste

Crayons

Number of Players:

Two

Preparation Directions:

1. Distribute copies of the activity sheets.

2. Provide pencils, scissors, paste, and crayons.

Player Directions:

1. Each player cuts out the names of the days of the week and the number cards.

2. The days and number cards are shuffled and placed face down.

3. The first player draws a card and asks the other player to spell a day of the week or a number that is written on it.

4. If the player spells the word correctly, he or she pastes the word in the correct space on the calendar.

5. The game continues until all of the words have been spelled and pasted on the calendar.

6. The players may use crayons to decorate the calendar.

7. The players use the calendar to answer the questions on the last activity.

Bonus Activity:

Direct students to use one of the following story starters to write a paragraph:

My favorite day of the week is . . .

Something I look forward to doing on Sunday is . . .

I will remember that Saturday because . . .

Monthly Madness Game Cards

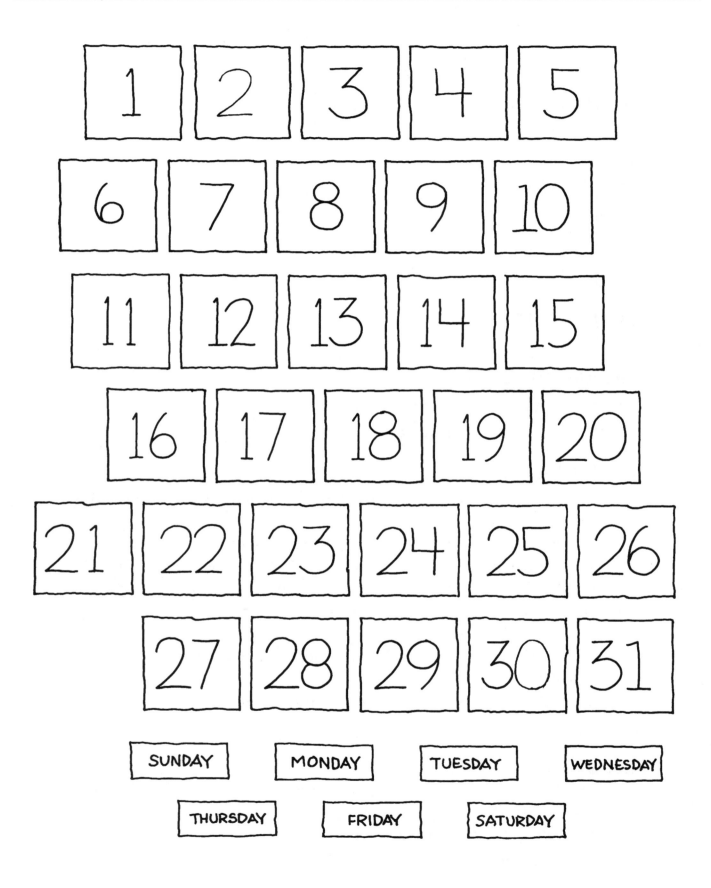

SUNDAY   MONDAY   TUESDAY   WEDNESDAY

THURSDAY   FRIDAY   SATURDAY

Monthly Madness Calendar

ESL Content-Based Language
Games, Puzzles, and Inventive Exercises

Monthly Madness Activity Sheet

1. My favorite day of the week is _____

   because _____

   _____

   _____

2. My favorite TV program is on this day: _____

3. What day is the first day of this month? _____

4. What day is the last day of this month? _____

5. What days in each week are school days?

   _____

   _____

   _____

   _____

   _____

6. Which day of the week has the most letters in its name?

   _____

7. How many days of the week begin with the letter "S"? _____

8. Which day of the week begins with the letter "W"? _____

9. What is the first day of the week? _____

   What is the last day of the week? _____

10. Write the abbreviations for the days of the week.

   _____ _____ _____

   _____ _____ _____

   _____

Fire!

Purpose:
Social Studies - fire prevention
Language: following directions, vocabulary development

Materials:
Copy of Alphabet Maze
Follow-up activity
Pencils
Crayons

Number of Players:
One or the entire class

Preparation Directions:
1. Distribute copies of the maze and the follow-up activity sheet.
2. Provide pencils and crayons

Player Directions:
1. The player or players follow the directions on the maze.
2. After completing the maze, the player or players follow the directions on the follow-up activity.

*ESL Content-Based Language
Games, Puzzles, and Inventive Exercises*

Fire!

Follow the maze to report a fire. Draw yourself using the telephone.

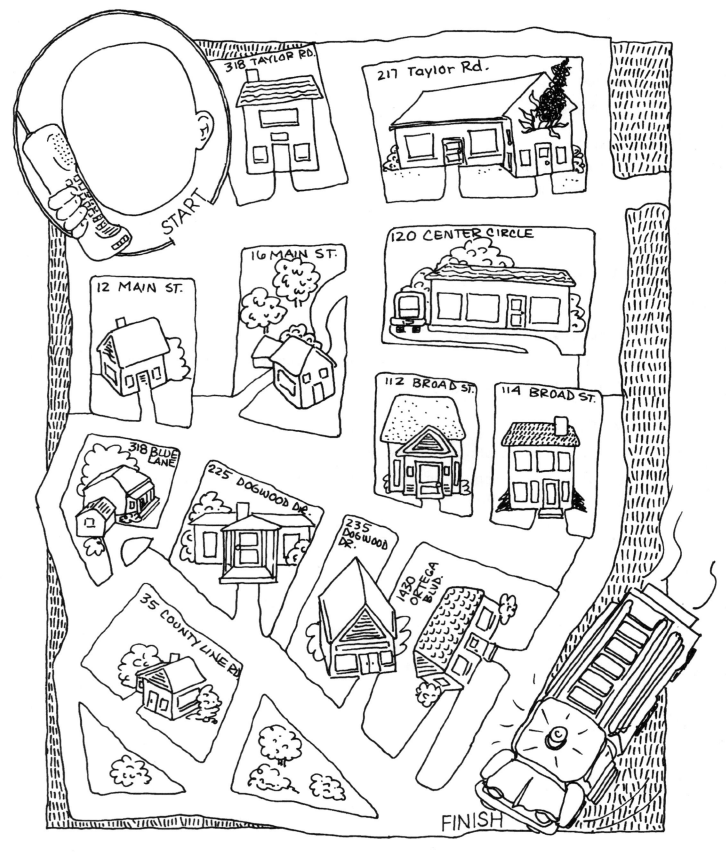

Fire! Follow-up Activity

Answer the following questions after you have completed the Fire! Maze activity.

1. The address of the fire is _____.

2. Is a house or an apartment on fire? _____

3. Draw and color a picture that shows one way to prevent a fire.

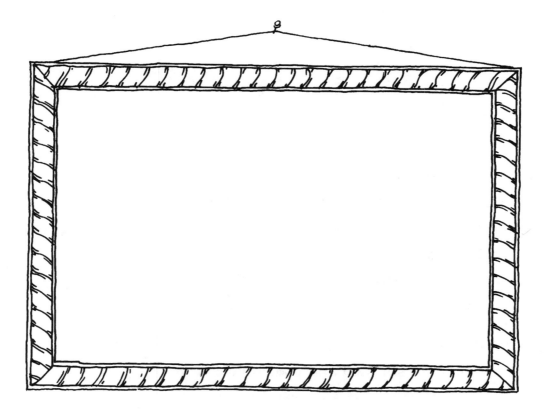

Now, complete the following sentences to show that you are ready to protect yourself from fire.

4. The telephone number to report a fire is _____.

5. Your telephone number is _____.

6. Your address is _____

_____

_____

ESL Content-Based Language
Games, Puzzles, and Inventive Exercises

Feelings

Purpose:

    Social Studies - emotions

    Language - group discussion, listening, speaking, word meaning, visualizing, drama

Materials:

    Copy of the game sheet

    Copy of the game cards

    Scissors

    Crayons

    Pencils

Number of Players:

    Two players

Preparation Directions:

1. Give each player a copy of the game sheet.
2. Cut out the game cards.
3. Provide pencils and crayons.
4. Lead a class discussion about emotions.
5. List the emotions on the chalkboard.

Player Directions:

1. The cards are shuffled and placed face down.
2. The first player draws and reads a card.
3. Then both players draw themselves showing this emotion on the correct face.
4. The players color the pictures.
5. Under each picture, the players write the name of the emotion in English and/or in their native language.

Bonus Activity:

Provide time for students to act out various emotions they have felt and ask class members to guess the emotion being portrayed. After the emotion has been correctly identified, allow the actor to explain the circumstances causing the emotion. Encourage other students to tell about times they have felt this same emotion. Guide the discussion to encourage the use of whole sentences and sequence of thought.

Feelings Game Sheet

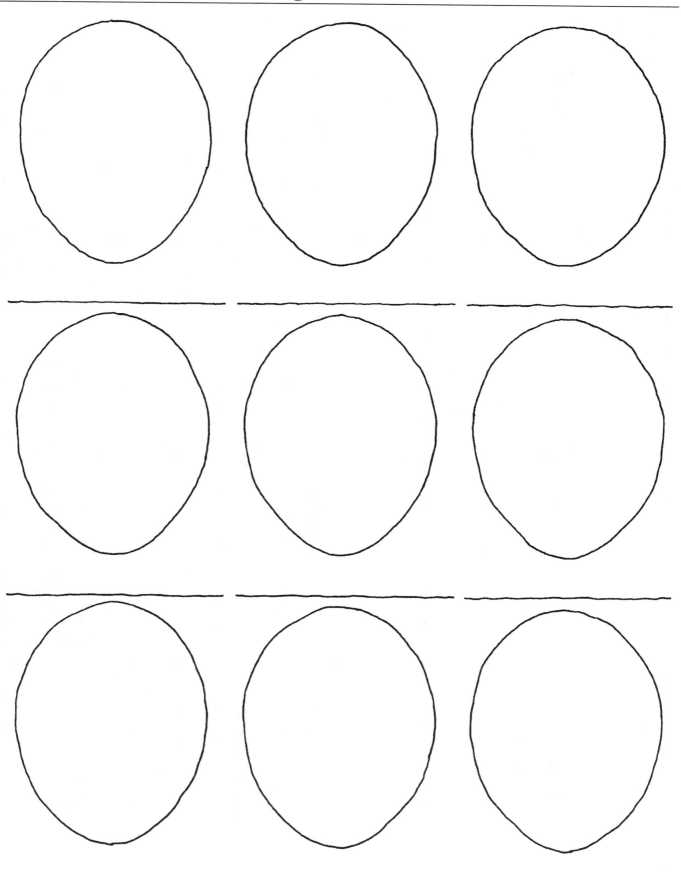

*ESL Content-Based Language
Games, Puzzles, and Inventive Exercises*

Feelings Game Cards

My grandmother is coming!

Eating a new food in your new country and you don't like it.

I am leaving my country.

I got a bad grade.

You are afraid of something.

It is the first day of school in my new country.

I met a new friend.

I got a new puppy!

It is my birthday and I got a gift!

I have been punished.

I am lost and I can't find my house.

I am sick.

Clothes Closet Countdown

Purpose:

    Social Studies - clothing

    Language - frequently used words, discussion, speaking, and listening

Materials:

    Copy of Puzzle

    Pencils

Number of Players:

    One or the entire class

Preparation Directions:

    1. Give each player a copy of the word search puzzle.

    2. Provide pencils.

Player Directions:

    1. The players circle all the names of clothing in the word search.

    2. Provide time for the players to share and discuss the answers.

R	A	I	N	C	O	A	T	R	Z	T	G
S	W	E	A	T	E	R	O	P	B	Q	L
H	P	B	H	J	N	M	M	E	K	B	O
O	O	D	T	-	S	H	I	R	T	L	V
E	F	G	S	L	H	A	N	B	Y	O	E
S	X	G	S	K	I	R	T	E	P	U	S
H	C	O	A	T	R	N	D	R	E	S	S
O	A	F	M	I	T	A	L	T	L	E	N
R	P	A	V	E	S	T	F	G	K	L	M
T	O	H	G	V	W	B	O	O	T	S	Z
S	Q	A	R	N	K	S	O	C	K	S	M
B	A	T	H	I	N	G	S	U	I	T	X
T	N	M	N	P	R	V	P	A	N	T	S
Z	J	A	C	K	E	T	A	D	T	K	I

Words to Find: T-SHIRT, COAT, TIE, SHIRT, BATHING SUIT, DRESS, SHOES, CAP, GLOVES, BLOUSE, BOOTS, SWEATER, VEST, JACKET, HAT, SHORTS, RAINCOAT, SKIRT, PANTS, SOCKS

Transportation Teasers

Purpose:

Social Studies - transportation

Language - word identification, discussion, speaking and listening, descriptive words

Materials:

Copy of word search

Copy of words to find in the word search

Pencils

Resource books

Number of Players:

Two

Preparation Directions:

1. Lead a class discussion of different means of transportation.

2. List the transportation names on the chalkboard.

3. Give each player a copy of the word search.

Player Directions:

1. The players circle all of the transportation words in the puzzle.

2. Divide students into cooperative learning groups to complete the word search puzzle.

3. Provide time for puzzles to be checked out and shared in a total group setting.

Bonus Activity:

Ask students to work together in groups of 2 or 3 to plan and complete a mural showing all the forms of transportation they have personally used. Provide time for student groups to share the completed murals with the total group. Encourage them to use colorful descriptive words and phrases to describe the vehicles in the mural. For example, the "enormous jet black car," instead of the "big black car."

Transportation Teasers Word Find

Circle the transportation words in the "Words to Find."

CART AUTOMOBILE DOGSLED ROCKET CAMEL MOTORCYCLE
DONKEY TRUCK SHIP CANOE ELEPHANT BUS
SCHOOL BUS SPACESHIP HELICOPTER WHEELCHAIR RAM
BIKE AMBULANCE WALKING HORSE SUBWAY TAXI
TRAIN CAR WAGON BOAT VAN AIRPLANE BALLOON JET

```
D  O  A  H  E  L  I  C  O  P  T  E  R  W
S  B  U  S  P  Q  S  C  T  S  H  I  P  H
P  O  A  C  A  R  T  A  X  I  S  E  T  E
A  A  I  D  U  A  S  R  E  D  C  L  C  E
C  T  R  F  T  M  G  J  K  P  H  E  A  L
E  S  P  D  O  G  S  L  E  D  O  P  N  C
S  U  L  T  M  E  E  J  P  O  O  H  O  H
H  B  A  R  O  C  K  E  T  N  L  A  E  A
I  W  N  T  B  L  F  T  R  K  B  N  T  I
P  A  E  M  I  L  T  O  U  E  U  T  B  R
W  Y  V  M  L  T  P  R  C  Y  S  X  I  T
A  C  A  M  E  L  A  M  K  E  T  Y  K  R
G  B  N  M  O  T  O  R  C  Y  C  L  E  A
O  A  M  B  U  L  A  N  C  E  A  U  Y  I
N  K  T  P  O  W  A  L  K  I  N  G  N  N
L  B  A  L  L  O  O  N  H  O  R  S  E  N
```

Scrambled Months

Purpose:
    Language Arts - spelling, abbreviations
    Social Studies - months of the year

Materials:
    Copy of the puzzle
    Pencils

Number of Players:
    A whole class

Preparation Directions:

1. Make a copy of the Scrambled Months puzzle for each student.

2. Divide the class into groups of two.

Player Directions:

1. A copy of the puzzle is given to each student.

2. At a given signal, ask each group to unscramble the letters that will spell the months of the year.

3. When a group completes the puzzle, they will stand up.

4. The teacher checks each group to see if the months are spelled correctly.

5. Then ask students to continue to work together to write the abbreviation for each month.

*ESL Content-Based Language
Games, Puzzles, and Inventive Exercises*

Scrambled Months Puzzle

1. AYM _ _ _

2. BROTECO _ _ _ _ _ _ _

3. UYJL _ _ _ _

4. RNJYAAU _ _ _ _ _ _ _

5. HACRM _ _ _ _ _

6. UTASGU _ _ _ _ _ _

7. EMREDBCE _ _ _ _ _ _ _ _

8. EUNJ _ _ _ _

9. SRPEEBTME _ _ _ _ _ _ _ _ _

10. RAIPL _ _ _ _ _

11. YFREABUR _ _ _ _ _ _ _ _

12. VMORNEBE _ _ _ _ _ _ _ _

JANUARY
July February   June   August   MARCH
October   NOVEMBER
MAY December   APRIL   September

Write the abbreviation for each month.

13. _____

14. _____

15. _____

16. _____

17. _____

18. _____

19. _____

20. _____

21. _____

22. _____

23. _____

24. _____

Weather Watch

Purpose:

Language Arts - vocabulary reinforcement, words in context, letter writing

Science - weather

Materials:

Weather Search Activity Sheet

Pencils

Number of Players:

One, small groups, or the entire class.

Preparation Directions:

1. Distribute copies of the weather watch game sheet.

2. Provide pencils.

Player Directions:

1. The Weather Search Game sheet is completed or compared and discussed in small groups.

Bonus Activity:

Ask students to write a letter to a friend describing their favorite month of the year. If a holiday, birthday, or other special event occurs in that month, ask them to be sure to describe it in detail. Review the parts of a personal letter before the writing exercise begins.

Weather Watch Game Sheet

Freezing   Thunder   Rainy   Hot
Lightning   Storm   Windy   Sunny
Warm   Chilly   Icy   Blustery
Snow   Cloudy

Complete the following sentences with words from the word box.

1. _ _ _ _ _ _ _ _ temperature is 32 degrees Fahrenheit.

2. It is nice to sit in the shade of a big tree on a _ _ _ summer day.

3. Spring brings _ _ _ _ sunny days and blue skies.

4. When _ _ _ _ _ _ _ _ _ flashes and _ _ _ _ _ _ _ roars, we know

   that a _ _ _ _ _ is on the way.

5. A _ _ _ _ _ day is the perfect time to fly a kite.

6. Sitting beside the fire place on a dark _ _ _ _ _ _ _ _ day is delightful.

7. Warm days and _ _ _ _ _ _ nights are signs of fall.

8. Nothing is more beautiful than trees and rooftops covered with

   new fallen _ _ _ _ .

9. We need umbrellas for _ _ _ _ _ days.

10. Drivers need to be extra careful when driving on _ _ _ slick roads.

11. Just before the storm, the sky turned dark and _ _ _ _ _ _ _ .

12. I hope we will have a bright _ _ _ _ _ day for our class picnic.

Sensibility

Purpose:

  Science - the five senses

Materials:

  Copy of game board
  Copy of game cards
  Game markers

Number of Players:

  Two, three, or four players

Preparation Directions:

  1. Distribute copies of the game board and game cards.

  2. Distribute a game marker to each player.

  3. Ask groups to cut out the game cards.

Player Directions:

  1. The game cards are shuffled and placed face down.

  2. The first player draws a card and reads it.

  3. If the player gives the correct answer to the question on the card, he or she moves one space.

  4. The other players then take turns drawing cards and answering the questions.

  5. The game continues until one player reaches "Finish" and wins the game.

ESL Content-Based Language
Games, Puzzles, and Inventive Exercises

Sensibility Game Cards

What
is
green?

What
is a
rectangle?

What
feels
furry?

What
is
bright?

What
is
long?

What
is a
quiet
sound?

What
is a
sound
at home?

What
is a
rain
sound?

What
feels
hot?

What
smells
good?

What
feels
smooth?

What
is
square?

*ESL Content-Based Language
Games, Puzzles, and Inventive Exercises*

Sensibility Game Cards Continued

What tastes salty?

What sounds loud?

What feels soft?

What feels hard?

What is round?

What tastes sour?

What feels rough?

What tastes sweet?

What feels wet?

What smells bad?

What tastes spicy?

What is a sound at school?

*ESL Content-Based Language
Games, Puzzles, and Inventive Exercises*

Sensibility Game Board

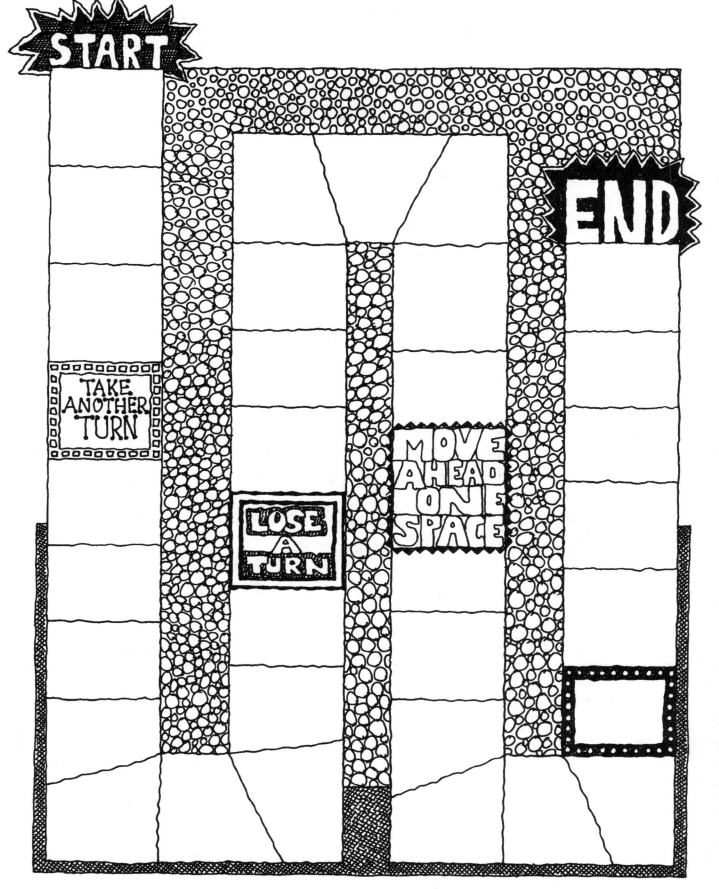

*ESL Content-Based Language
Games, Puzzles, and Inventive Exercises*

Body Parts

Purpose:

   Science - body parts

   Language Arts - word meaning and usage, active listening,
   following directions

Materials:

   Copy of Puzzle
   Pencils

Number of Players:

   One or the entire class

Preparation Directions:

   1. Give each player a copy of the word search puzzle.

   2. Provide pencils.

Player Directions:

   1. The players circle all the names of body parts in the word search.

   2. After completing the game, the players share the answers.

Bonus Activity:

Play "Simon Says" or some other interactive game requiring students to
identify body parts.

Rules for "Simon Says": The players stand in a row, facing the caller. The
caller pronounces and acts out directions asking players to touch body
parts as they are named. Example: "Simon says touch your stomach".
When "Simon says" precedes the directions, the players follow the
directions. As the game progresses and the tempo gets faster, the caller
occasionally omits "Simon Says". If a player touches the body part when
this happens, he or she is out of the game and sits down. The last player
left standing is the winner of the game.

Parts of the Body Word Search

WRIST	LEG	ELBOW	TEETH	HAND	TONGUE	NECK

LIPS   EAR   NOSE   EYE   MOUTH

ARM   KNEE   FOOT   SHOULDER   HEAD   CHEEK

HAIR   EYEBROW   TOE   FINGER   HEEL

```
A C Z Q R V X T O E M B
L K O R G F T Y H A N D
C P T E E T H A I R N N
B N O K L W M R N P R W
F I N G E R W M N N K E
L E G Y L I X L H E E L
Z R U A B S O U T M J A
N K E N O T M N N E C K
N B J O W I O M L Y J D
G R A S H O U L D E R P
K N E E E F T H B B W R
Q U N K A R H T S R S B
W L Y O D E M I F O O T
N I G T E Y N N E W S E
E P C H E E K C O L K A
N S A S I W A H J D B M
```

Foods to Find

Purpose:

    Science - foods

    Language Arts - vocabulary, discussion

Materials:

    Copy of Puzzle

    Pencils

Number of Players:

    One or the entire class

Preparation Directions:

1. Give each player a copy of the word search puzzle.

2. Provide pencils.

Player Directions:

1. The players circle all the names of animals, foods, body parts, or clothing in the word searches.

2. Provide time for the players to share and discuss their answers.

Foods to Find Words to Find

MEAT   SPAGHETTI   BEANS   GRAPES   BREAD   RICE
SOUP   EGG   CEREAL   BANANA   CHICKEN   JUICE   POTATO
FISH   MILK   PIZZA   APPLE   HAMBURGER   ORANGE
SALAD   ICE CREAM   TACO   CHIPS   NUTS

Y F I S H P G R A P E S S
N U T S X B R E A D Q A
T N B P U R N S T T O L
W H H A M B U R G E R A
P Y T G B E R E G N A D
O E E H F A K L M O N V
T V A E L N A S P E G U
A F I T N S J U I C E M
T A A T N F W B F B L Y
O C H I C E C R E A M U
A P P L E R N B G N U P
T C H I C K E N G A M I
T H E R A B M R E N I Z
R I C E A C E R E A L Z
D P F O B R A E A K K A
F S O U P A T A C O S T

Season Search

Purpose:

> **Science** - seasons
>
> **Math** - counting
>
> **Language Arts** - picture and word association, main idea

Materials:

> Copy of season activity sheets
>
> Pencils
>
> Crayons

Number of Players:

> Individual Activity

Preparation Directions:

> 1. Lead a class discussion to review the four seasons.
>
> 2. Distribute the activity sheets.
>
> 3. Provide pencils and crayons.

Player Directions:

> 1. Using "Activity 1", the students count by ones to connect the dots to find the season, and then write the name of the season under the picture.
>
> 2. Using "Activity 2", the students count by twos to connect the dots to find the season, and then they write the name of the season under the picture.
>
> 3. "Activity 3" is completed in the same way except the students count by fives.
>
> 4. "Activity 4" is completed by counting by tens.
>
> 5. Ask students to color the seasonal pictures with colors appropriate to the season.

What is this season?

What is this season?

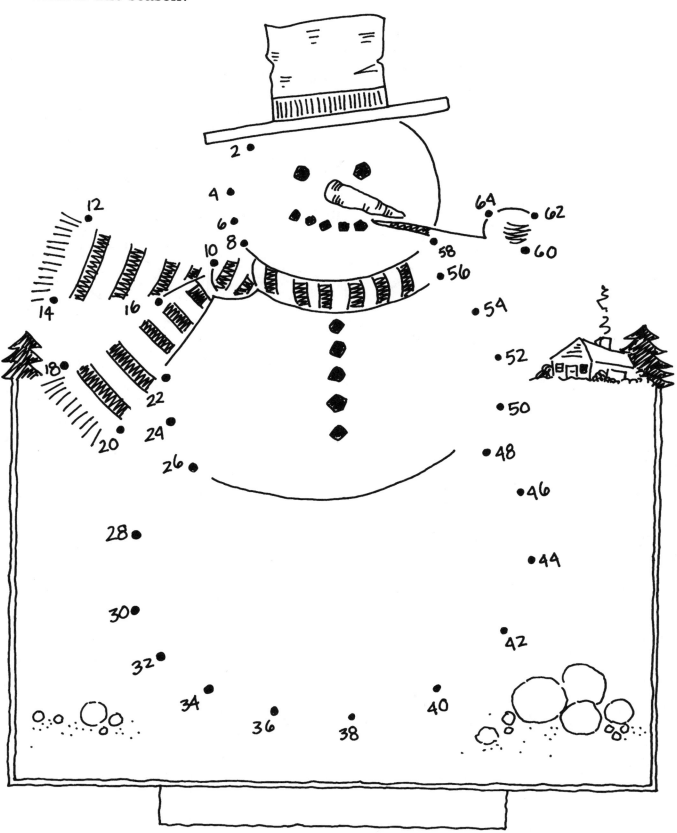

Season Search Activity 3

What is this season?

ESL Content-Based Language
Games, Puzzles, and Inventive Exercises

Season Search Activity 4

What is this season?

*ESL Content-Based Language
Games, Puzzles, and Inventive Exercises*

Fun at the Farm

Purpose:

Science - animals

Language Arts - word identification, drama

Materials:

Copy of Puzzle

Pencils

Number of Players:

One or the entire class

Preparation Directions:

1. Distribute copies of the word search puzzle.

2. Provide pencils.

Player Directions:

1. The players circle all the names of animals in the word search.

2. Time is provided for the players to share their answers.

3. A discussion is conducted to focus on each animal's usefulness to the farmer, and the products that may be derived from the animals.

4. A game entitled "What Animal Am I ?" will reinforce concepts gained and provide opportunity for use of basic language skills. Have students work together in groups of 3 or 4 to act out the behavior of the animal, make the sound the animal makes, and ask the class to guess what animal they are portraying. Information gained may be processed and retained within a more meaningful concept.

Fun at the Farm

DUCK   PIG   DOG   HORSE

GOAT   DONKEY   CAT

HEN   COW   CALF   PONY

```
R G O A T N R
D O G F Z H Q
U H O R S E P
C A T S B N O
K J C A L F N
R D O N K E Y
T V W P I G R
```

ESL Content-Based Language
Games, Puzzles, and Inventive Exercises

Animal Hide and Seek

Purpose:

    Science - animals and their habitats

    Language Arts - following directions, vocabulary development, using resource materials, and visualization

Materials:

    Copy of Maze

    Follow-up activity sheets

    Pencils

    Crayons

Number of Players:

    One or the entire class

Preparation Directions:

1. Distribute copies of the maze and copies of the follow-up activity sheets.
2. Provide pencils and crayons
3. Lead a class discussion about animals and their habitats.
4. Provide resource books.

Player Directions:

1. The player or players follow the directions on the maze.
2. After completing the maze, the player or players are asked to draw and color each animal found in a designated habitat.
3. As a culminating activity, time should be provided for a discussion on the completed activity sheets.

Animal Hide and Seek

Follow the maze to help the zookeeper find and name the animals.

ESL Content-Based Language Games, Puzzles, and Inventive Exercises

Animal Hide and Seek Activity

Draw the following animals and their habitats in the squares.

cat	monkey
turtle	spider
pig	lion

Animal Hide and Seek Activity Continued

Draw the following animals and their habitats in the squares.

fish	camel
snake	bird
horse	dog

ESL Content-Based Language
Games, Puzzles, and Inventive Exercises

Language Skills Matrix

	Vocabulary	Speaking	Decision Making	Writing & Reading	Discussion & Listening	5 Senses	Following Directions	Rhyming Descriptive Words	Main Idea & Titles	Locating Information	Word Recognition & Abbreviations	Visualizing
Content Focus: Math												
Time on the Line	+	+	+									
Pizza Problems				+	+							
Orange Orchard				+			+	+				
Odd & Even Jelly Beans					+		+					
Space Craft				+			+					
A Visit to the Zoo				+			+					
Calendar Clues	+									+		
Number Land				+								
Hamburger House	+			+			+					
Content Focus: Social Studies												
Sign Savvy	+										+	
Monthly Madness				+							+	
Fire!	+						+					
Feelings		+			+						+	+
Clothes Closet Countdown		+			+						+	
Transportation Teasers		+			+						+	
Scrambled Months	+										+	
Weather Watch	+			+							+	
Sensibility						+						
Content Focus: Science												
Body Parts					+		+				+	
Foods to Find	+				+						+	
Season Search									+		+	
Animal Fun at the Farm	+										+	
Animal Hide and Seek	+				+		+			+		+

ESL Content-Based Language
Games, Puzzles, and Inventive Exercises

Annotated Bibliography
for the ESL Teacher

BASIC/Not Boring Reading Comprehension, Grades 4-5. Imogene Forte and Marjorie Frank. Nashville, Incentive Publications, Inc., 1998
Imaginative activities covering essential reading skills such as: main ideas, finding information, sequencing, and paraphrasing.

BASIC/Not Boring Spelling, Grades 4-5, Imogene Forte and Marjorie Frank. Nashville, Incentive Publications, Inc., 1999
Imaginative activities covering essential spelling skills such as: identifying correctly spelled and misspelled words, learning the "ie" rules, and distinguishing among homophones.

BASIC/Not Boring Reading, Grades 2-3. Imogene Forte and Marjorie Frank. Nashville, Incentive Publications, Inc., 1998
Imaginative activities covering essential reading skills such as: main idea, sequencing, charts, directions, and characters.

BASIC/Not Boring Spelling, Grades 2-3. Imogene Forte and Marjorie Frank. Nashville, Incentive Publications, Inc. 2000
Imaginative activities covering essential spelling skills such as: compound words, consonant blends, and frequently misspelled words.

The Cooperative Learning Guide and Planning Pak for the Primary Grades. Imogene Forte and Joy MacKenzie. Nashville, Incentive Publications, Inc., 1992
Includes an overview of cooperative learning and thematic teaching, content mini-units, interdisciplinary units, and thematic learning stations.

Cooperative Learning Teacher Timesavers. Imogene Forte. Nashville, Incentive Publications, Inc., 1992
Contains summaries, warm-ups, bulletin boards, and cooperative activities, and motivational ideas, as well as ready-to-use reproducible aids, badges, clip art, reports, worksheets, and records.

Creating Connection: Learning to Appreciate Diversity. Dorothy Michener. Nashville, Incentive Publications, Inc., 1995
Provides practical strategies and workable solutions for educators striving to help their students recognize, understand, and appreciate diversity.

Easy Art Projects to Teach Global Awareness. Lynn Brisson. Nashville, Incentive Publications, Inc., 1993
Topics covered include map skills, the 50 United States, the 7 continents, desert and ocean study, and more!

ESL Active Learning Lessons: 15 Complete Content-Based Units to Reinforce Language Skills and Concepts. Imogene Forte and Mary Ann Pangle. Nashville, Incentive Publications, Inc., 2001
Provides practice and reinforcement in the use of listening, speaking, reading and writing.

ESL Reading and Spelling Games, Puzzles, and Inventive Exercises. Imogene Forte and Mary Ann Pangle. Nashville, Incentive Publications, Inc., 2001
Offers useable guides to learn, practice, and master a variety of language-based skills, focusing on reading and spelling.

ESL Vocabulary and Word Usage Games, Puzzles, and Inventive Exercises. Imogene Forte and Mary Ann Pangle. Nashville, Incentive Publications, Inc., 2001
Offers useable guides to learn, practice, and master a variety of language-based skills, focusing on vocabulary and word usage.

Hands-On Math. Kathleen Fletcher. Nashville, Incentive Publications, Inc., 1996
Contains all the essentials and extras for teaching number-sense concepts. Included ideas for using stamps, stickers, beans, rice, tiles, and number lines and manipulatives in the classroom.

Internet Quest. Catherine Halloran Cook and Janet McGivney Pfeifer. Nashville, Incentive Publications, Inc., 2000
Designed to engage students in learning on the web. 101 new sites to explore covering exciting topics such as: art and music, geography and travel, nature and science.

Language Arts Folder Fun. Kathy Blankenhorn and Joanne Richards. Nashville, Incentive Publications, Inc., 1995
Folder games target and reinforce the fundamentals of language arts.

Learning to Learn: Strengthening Study Skills and Brain Power. Gloria Frender. Nashville, Incentive Publications, Inc., 1990
Includes step-by-step procedures for improving organizational skills, time management, problem solving, power reading, test taking, memory skills, and more!

Multicultural Plays: A Many-Splendored Tapestry Honoring Our Global Community. Judy Mecca. Nashville, Incentive Publications, Inc., 1999
Easily-produced plays allow students to learn about and develop respect for different cultures. A brief cultural lesson accompanies each play to ensure an authentic performance.

On the Loose With Dr. Seuss. Shirley Cook. Nashville, Incentive Publications, Inc., 1994
Each literature-based unit includes background information about Dr. Seuss and one of his stories, extended thinking and writing exercises, and special imaginative activities.

Reading Reinforcers for the Primary Grades. Imogene Forte. Nashville, Incentive Publications, Inc., 1994
A collection of teacher-directed interactive projects, creative worksheets, and independent and group activities.

Seasonal Activities for Classroom Creativity. Kitty Hazler. Nashville, Incentive Publications, Inc., 1999
High-interest lessons to nurture creativity and promote higher order thinking skills within a seasonal theme. Students gain fluency and originality.

Using Literature to Learn About Children Around the World. Judith Cochran. Nashville, Incentive Publications, Inc., 1993
Lesson plans outline specific activities to develop social and global awareness and to strengthen vocabulary and thinking skills.

Answer Key

Page 13

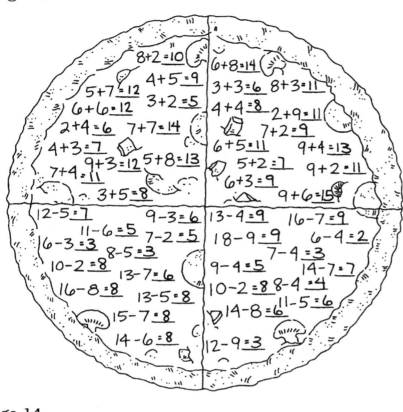

Page 14

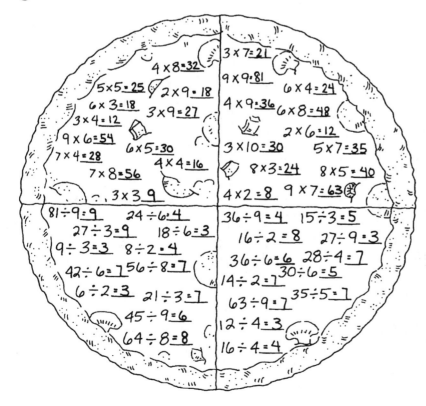

Page 17

1. 14 - 1 ten 4 ones
2. 27 - 2 tens 7 ones
3. 31 - 3 tens 1 ones
4. 20 - 2 tens 0 ones
5. 19 - 1 ten 9 ones
6. 42 - 4 tens 2 ones
7. 16 - 1 ten 6 ones
8. 9 - 0 tens 9 ones
9. 28 - 2 tens 8 ones
10. 34 - 3 tens 4 ones

Page 37

1–5. Answers will vary.
6. Wednesday
7. seven
8. nine
9. Answers will vary.
10. Sun.
Mon.
Tues.
Wed.
Thurs.
Fri.
Sat.

Page 43

1. 217 Taylor Road
2. house
3–6. Answers will vary.

ESL Content-Based Language
Games, Puzzles, and Inventive Exercises

Page 48

Page 50

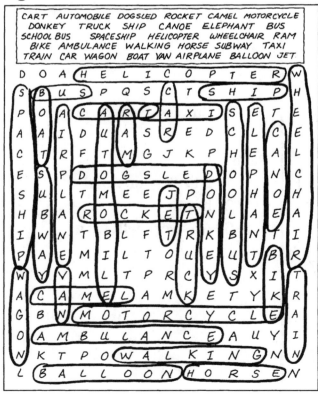

Page 52

1. May	9. September	17. May
2. October	10. April	18. Jun.
3. July	11. February	19. Jul.
4. January	12. November	20. Aug.
5. March	13. Jan.	21. Sept.
6. August	14. Feb.	22. Oct.
7. December	15. Mar.	23. Nov.
8. June	16. Apr.	24. Dec.

Page 54

1. Freezing	5. Windy	10. Icy
2. Hot	6. Blustery	11. Cloudy
3. Warm	7. Chilly	12. Sunny
4. Lightning, thunder, storm	8. Snow	
	9. Rainy	

Page 60

MEAT	SPAGHETTI	BEANS	GRAPES	BREAD	RICE
SOUP	EGG	CEREAL	BANANA	CHICKEN	JUICE	POTATO
FISH	MILK	PIZZA	APPLE	HAMBURGER	ORANGE
SALAD	ICE CREAM	TACO	CHIPS	NUTS

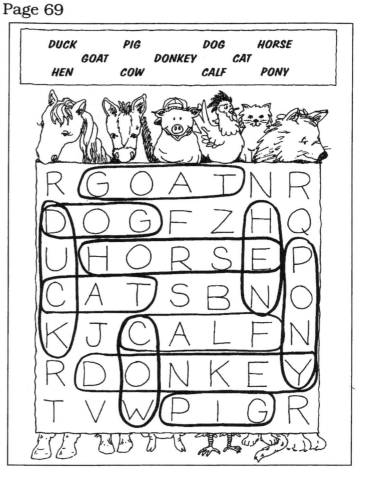

DUCK	PIG	DOG	HORSE
GOAT	DONKEY	CAT
HEN	COW	CALF	PONY

Page 64

Summer

Page 65

Winter

Page 66

Fall

Page 67

Spring